WRITTEN by LInda CooPeR

ILLUSTRATED by JAna VUKOVIĆ

Lenny and Nina

ARE BURIED IH BOOKS

Published by **Library Juice Press**
P.O. Box 188784
Sacramento, CA 95818

www.libraryjuicepress.com

Printed on acid-free, sustainably-sourced paper

ISBN: 978-1-936117-88-8

Nina

Lenny

Lenny and Nina had a LOT of books. They liked books. And so did their parents and grandparents and aunts and uncles and friends. They gave Lenny and Nina many, many books and the books were all well read and well loved. But things were getting out of hand.

"Lenny, have you seen the book with the red bird?" said Nina.

"No, I haven't. Have you seen the book about magic tricks?" said Lenny.

"Sorry," said Nina.

"We really need to do something about this," said Lenny. "We have so many books we cannot find anything. Maybe we should throw some of them out."

"No!" said Nina. "We need to think of something else."

Just then there was a knock on the door. It was Grandma.

Lenny opened the door and she came in. "Where is Nina?" said Grandma.

"Here I am," said Nina. She was hidden behind a huge pile of books.

"My, you do have a lot of books," said Grandma.

"I think we have too many," said Lenny. "They are all over. There are so many that we can't find the books we are looking for."

"Maybe it is time to **organize** your books into a **library**," said Grandma.

TO **ORGANIZE** MEANS TO SET UP THINGS IN A SPECIAL WAY.

A **LIBRARY** IS A PLACE WHERE BOOKS ARE KEPT IN A WAY SO THAT ARE EASY TO FIND.

Of course Lenny and Nina had been to their public library and their school library but they never thought of making their own library at home.

"How can we do that?" asked Nina. "Well," said Grandma, "first maybe you should think of what it is that a library does for people. What do you want yours to do for you?"

"I want to be able to find my red bird book when I want it," said Nina.

"OK," said Grandma, "think about other things you need to find every day that are not books. How do you know where to find your green sweater when you want it?"

"Well, Mom puts all my sweaters in one drawer – the sweater drawer – and I know if I look there, that is where it should be. And all my socks are in the sock drawer and all my underwear is in the underwear drawer. Each thing has its own drawer."

"How about other things," said Grandma. "How do you find the food you want in a supermarket? A supermarket is huge. How do you find the kind of tomato sauce you are looking for?"

"Well," said Lenny, "each aisle has certain things in it. We go to the aisle with all the different tomato sauces and then we can look for the one we want. If we want cookies, we look in the cookie aisle."

"So," said Grandma, "you can do the same thing with your books. You can **sort** them. That means to put things together that are the same in some way."

supermarket

TO SORT MEANS TO PUT THINGS TOGETHER THAT ARE ALIKE in SOME WAY.

Lenny and Nina began sorting their books. Any books about birds went in one pile. Books about dogs went in another pile. Fairy tales, trucks, magic, soccer – each had their own pile.

"If my favorite book is about a red bird," asked Nina, "does it go with books about birds or does it go with books about red?"

"Ah!" said Grandma. "That is something you have to decide yourself. This is your library!"

Nina decided to have a pile of books that had mostly to do with colors – red birds, blue sky, yellow flowers – because the colors were very important to her. That way she could look in her color pile whenever she wanted to look at a book about a color.

"These piles are too high," said Lenny. "They are going to get knocked down."

So Mom cleared off a book shelf for the children and they put each pile of books on a shelf. Since there were more piles than shelves, some small piles shared a shelf.

Then they made little labels with the name of each shelf and taped it to the shelf. There was a shelf called COLORS and a shelf called MAGIC and a shelf called DOGS and many other shelves.

"Now we have our library!" said Nina.

Nina got so excited that she spilled her juice on her red bird book and it was ruined.

"Don't be sad," said Grandma. "Let's go to the **public library** and see if they have a copy."

A PUBLIC LIBRARY

IS A LIBRARY THAT IS USED BY EVERYONE IN THE COMMUNITY.

⑨

The children had been to the public library many times, but this time, since they had just made their own library at home, the really noticed how many hundreds and hundreds of books were on the shelves.

"Wow," said Lenny. "It must have been really hard to sort all of these. There are so many!"

"Where is the shelf for 'red,'" said Nina. She wanted to find the book about a red bird.

"Well," said Grandma, "in this library, there will not be a shelf for red. This library is used by many, many people. The books need to be sorted in a way that will help most people find what they want. Most people will not look for a shelf about red to find a book about a red bird. They will look on a shelf with bird books."

"Who gets to decide how to organize the books and what the shelves will be called?" asked Lenny. "Well," said Grandma, "since there are so many people who use this library, they all had to agree on one way to sort books. A long time ago a man named Melvil Dewey made up a system, a way of doing this. His system has a fancy name. It is called the **Dewey Decimal System** and it is the way most public libraries organize their books."

THE
DEWEY DECIMAL SYSTEM

Melvil Dewey

IS THE SPECIAL WAY THAT BOOKS ARE ORGANIZED IN A LIBRARY.

⑪

0 0 0 0 0 0 0 0

Mr. Dewey tried to think of all the different groups or categories that books might go into. Each book would be put into the **category** that the book is most about and that most people would understand.

A **CATEGORY** IS A GROUP OF THINGS THAT ARE ALIKE IN SOME WAY.

ART HISTORY TEHNOLOGY SCIENCE

"But there are so many books here," said Nina. "How will I ever find the book about a red bird that I want?"

"We will look in the library catalog," said Grandma. A **catalog** is a list or collection of things that people might want to find. Sometimes there is a little description of each thing or a picture of it to help the reader know whether that is what she wants. Your family may receive catalogs of clothes or toys or tools in the mail. In the library, there is a catalog that helps people find books. This catalog is kept on a computer. Let's ask the librarian if she can help us.

A CATALOG

IS A BOOK OR LIST OF THINGS
THAT PEOPLE MIGHT WANT TO FIND.

CATALOG
1.
2.
3.
4.
5.

They found the librarian who was very happy to show them the library catalog. "To find the book you want," she said, "we need to know something about it like the name of the book or who wrote the book or what it is about. "

"The book I want is about a red bird," said Nina. "There is a picture of it on the cover of the book and it is book for children." "OK," said the librarian. "First let's type the word Bird into the computer." Many book titles appeared on the computer screen. "Now let's tell the computer that this is a children's book." This time far fewer names appeared. "I think the name of the book is Cardinals," said Lenny. The librarian put that name into the computer and one book came up.

"Hurray!" said Nina, "but how do we know where to find it? There are so many shelves."

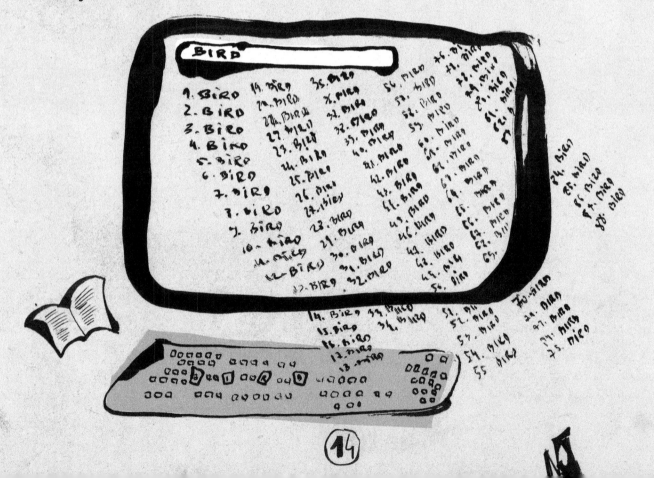

"Each book has its own special number," said the librarian. "Sort of like an address. When someone comes to visit you at your home, your mom or dad gives them directions. First they need to know where your neighborhood is. Then they need to know your street name and house number. They need to know your address to find you. Each book has its own address or **call number**. You will see the call number of each book on the bottom edge of the book when it is lined up on the shelf with all the others."

A CALL NUMBER

IS THE SPECIAL NUMBER ON A BOOK THAT TELLS WHERE IT CAN BE FOUND IN THE LIBRARY.

In the same way that each street in your neighborhood has a name or number, and each house has its own number, each shelf in the library has a number and then each book on the shelf has its own special number. The librarian wrote down the call number of the Cardinal book on a small piece of paper.

"The children's book section is over here," said the librarian, leading the way. "The bird books are on the shelf with the number 598. Can you find the call number we are looking for on this shelf?"

Nina looked at the edge of each book carefully. The edge of a book is called the **spine** of the book. It is sort of like the spine on the back of a person. It helps keep the back of the book nice and straight. The spine of a book is where the call number is found.

"Here is the number," said Nina. "Let's see if it is the book I want." She pulled the book from the shelf and – hurray! – she had found her red bird book. "Can I take it home now?" she asked.

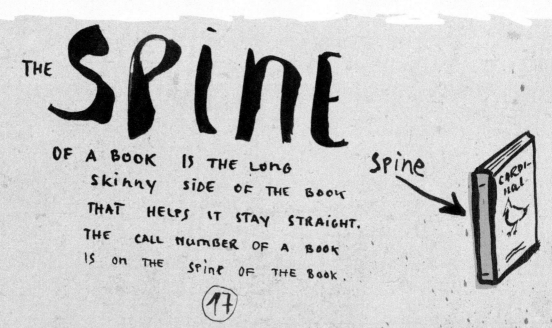

THE SPINE

OF A BOOK IS THE LONG SKINNY SIDE OF THE BOOK THAT HELPS IT STAY STRAIGHT. THE CALL NUMBER OF A BOOK IS ON THE SPINE OF THE BOOK.

Spine

"Of course," said the librarian. "We just need to check it out." "What does that mean?" said Nina. "Come over here to our desk," said the librarian. Grandma gave the librarian her library card. "My library card lets me borrow books from the library," said Grandma. "When I am done reading them, I bring them back so other people can have a turn. All the people in the community share the library books together."

A LIBRARY CARD

IS A SPECIAL CARD
THAT ALLOWS PEOPLE
TO BORROW BOOKS
FROM THE PUBLIC LIBRARY.

GRANDMA'S LIBRARY CARD

The librarian took Grandma's library card and turned it over. She pointed at some lines in a little bar shaped rectangle. "This is called a bar code," said the librarian. "Each person's library card has its own special bar code. People cannot read bar codes but the computer can. If we hold the bar code under the computer's scanner, the computer can tell who is borrowing a book." Then she took the Cardinal book and pointed to a bar code on the back cover of the book. "Each book has its own bar code, too," she said. "If we scan the book's bar code now, the computer will remember the name of the book and the person who borrowed it. That way we can keep track of who borrows which books and if you forget to bring it back, we can remind you. That way other people can have a turn to read the book, too."

A BAR CODE

IS A SET OF LINES THAT A COMPUTER CAN READ. IN THE LIBRARY A BAR CODE TELLS THE NAMES OF BOOKS AND THE PEOPLE WHO BORROW THEM.

The librarian checked the book out and Lenny, Nina, and Grandma thanked her and went home. When they got home, Grandma read the Cardinal book with Nina and Lenny organized his toy trucks so they would be easy to find.

CPSIA information can be obtained
at www.ICGtesting.com
Printed in the USA
LVOW02s1557090816
499662LV00008B/21/P

642-3